MW00654509

CAPE TOWN
Then and Now

DEDICATED TO
Kerry, Emma and Aeryn

CAPE TOWN

Then and Now

Vincent van Graan

CLOCK TOWER

Clock Tower, V&A Waterfront

CONTENTS

ACKNOWLEDGEMENTS

Putting this book together was a great adventure and an amazing learning experience, and would not have happened without a group of very talented people. It gives me great pleasure to acknowledge those who made it possible.

Phil Massie, you are a great friend and photographer. Without your attention to detail and perfectionist way of working, this book would not have happened. Thank you for always making time in your hectic schedule and for sharing my vision.

Anne Clarkson, thank you for all your research and writing. I will miss our meetings at the Archives and your emails about the interesting things you discovered. This book belongs to you as much as anybody else.

My thanks to the staff at the Western Cape Archives and Records Service – Erika Le Roux, Achmat Smith, Ebrahim Kenny and Lunette Lourens – for making the research at the Archives such a pleasure. You were always willing to help and to go the extra mile without question. Without your help, this book would have taken a few more years to complete.

A special thank you to Jaco van der Merwe: since day one, more than ten years ago, you have been behind me and supported my ideas. Without your enthusiasm, this book would never have been. You are a great asset to the Archives and I think you are the only person who might love these old photographic collections more than I do.

To the team at The Aerial Perspective – Anthony Allen, Keith Quixley, Lucia Bellairs – your beautiful aerial photographs added the finishing touches that I needed. It's always a pleasure working with such talented professionals.

At Random House Struik, my thanks go to Pippa Parker and Janice Evans, for seeing and believing. You and your production team – managing editor Roelien Theron, editor Alfred LeMaitre and editorial assistant Alana Bolligelo – were fantastic to work with.

Thanks to Mike Ormrod, not just for keeping me employed all these years, but also for always helping with, and supporting, my sometimes obsessive fascination with old glass plates and photographs.

And, last but not least, thanks to Seppi Hochfellner, for added inspiration.

Vincent Rokitta van Graan

FOREWORD

My interest in photography began at an early age. My father was an amateur photographer, and, although he gave up his darkroom when I was very young, the enlargers, developing trays and chemicals made a big impression on me.

After completing a three-year BTech Diploma in photography at the Pretoria Technikon, I moved to Cape Town in 2001. I had the impression that there would be lots of overseas and local photographers looking for assistants, and that this would be a great way to gain work experience. After working as an assistant and freelance photographer for a while, I became more involved in the editing and printing side of the photographic process, and started working for a professional photography laboratory in the city. I specialise in large-format photographic printing that combines the traditional darkroom with the technology of modern digital photography. I am able to produce some of the highest-quality photographic prints in South Africa, and I work with a range of artists and photographers from all over the world. Together we print everything from full exhibitions and installations to one-off, limited-edition archival-quality photographs. Even though I do not get much time for my own photography any more, there is nothing else I would rather be doing, and I dread the day when my darkroom and chemicals finally become obsolete.

Since the first time I saw a glass-plate negative, I have been fascinated by the process. The photographers of the past had to have great patience to produce a photograph. Anybody who has ever used an 8 x 10-inch or 4 x 5-inch bellows camera will tell you not only how difficult they are to use, but also that the quality they produce is better than that of most modern digital cameras. I have been trying to buy and build up a collection of glass plates of my own. I go to antique markets and shops and am constantly on the lookout for where I might find more. However, most of the plates I find are badly damaged and faded from poor storage and exposure to light.

Some years ago, while doing research at the Western Cape Archives and Records Service, I came across the most beautifully photographed and best-preserved photographic collections I had ever seen. The quality of these photographs, especially the work of Arthur Elliott, Edward Steer and Thomas Ravenscroft, is on par with the best photographic images produced today. I decided then that I wanted to produce a book showcasing some of these photographs of Cape Town, combined with images of what these landscapes look like today.

Cape Town is one of the most beautiful cities in the world, and the backdrop of Table Mountain and the Peninsula make it ideal for such a comparison. In many cases, using the mountain as a reference, it is possible to find almost the exact spot where these old masters of photography set up their large cameras.

Precious few of the photographs and plates in the Archives are dated, but in most cases it was possible to determine more or less when they were taken from where they are in the collections or by comparing them with those that do have dates. Most of the photographs in the book were taken between circa 1880 and circa 1930, although there are a few, like the ones of the Roeland Street jail (now the Western Cape Archives and Records Service), from the 1970s.

After retouching and working with these photographs for years, I enjoy them more than ever, and I hope that every reader will appreciate how fortunate we are to have such a beautiful collection of photographs.

VINCENT ROKITTA VAN GRAAN
vrvangraan@yahoo.com

PHOTOGRAPH COLLECTIONS IN THE WESTERN CAPE ARCHIVES

The Western Cape Archives and Records Service, formerly known as the Cape Archives, preserves a number of important historical collections of photographs dating back to the late nineteenth century. This book includes numerous works from the collections of the photographers described below.

ARTHUR ELLIOTT was born in America in 1870 and grew up in great poverty. He made his way to South Africa in the 1890s, initially trying to make a living in Johannesburg. He fled to Cape Town at the time of the Second Anglo-Boer War (1899–1902), and it was then that a remarkable stroke of luck led to him embarking on a photographic career.

A friend gave him a quarter-plate camera, and he began photographing Boer prisoners at the prisoner-of-war camp in Green Point. His photographs were popular, and he made a good living selling prints. Encouraged, he opened a studio in Long Street, where he remained for most of his working life.

Elliott was particularly interested in the history of the Cape and its architecture, and his many photographs of picturesque scenes record much that was soon to disappear.

Arthur Elliott (1870–1938)

A number of exhibitions of his work were staged, the first during the Union celebrations of 1910. His second exhibition in 1913 was entitled 'The Story of South Africa told in 800 pictures', and the subject of the third exhibition in 1926 was 'Old Cape Colony'. His last exhibition, in 1930, was the most ambitious and contained over a thousand photographs.

Elliott's offer, shortly before his death on 22 November 1938, to sell his collection of photographs to the government for £5 000 was turned down, but in 1940 the Historical Monuments Commission bought the main collection for £2 525. The Western Cape Archives and Records Service in Cape Town acquired these photographs and negatives in 1946, where they remain to this day – a priceless record of the past.

HENRY CHARLES HOPKINS was born at Heidelberg, in the Cape Province, on 3 April 1918. He studied theology at the University of Stellenbosch, after which he ministered to various Dutch Reformed congregations in the Cape, and later served as a military chaplain.

Hopkins earned a Master's degree in History and had a great interest in genealogy. This led to his appointment as archivist to the Dutch Reformed Church in 1973. Eleven years later, he and his wife retired to the coastal town of Betty's Bay.

He was a great collector of books and photographs. A collection of his papers and research notes is held by the National Library of South Africa, in Cape Town. In 1992 Hopkins donated his photographs to the Archives, to be known as the Hopkins Collection. He died on 20 November 1992.

EDWARD JAMES STEER was born at Maidstone, Kent, in 1863. When he left school he was apprenticed to a chemist and druggist. The Steer family (father, mother and children) settled in Cape Town, probably circa 1880. In 1883 Edward Steer was examined by the Medical Board of the Cape and licensed to practise in the Colony.

He became interested in photography and astronomy as a young man, and at the inaugural meeting of the Cape Astronomical Association in 1912 was elected Librarian. Later he became Treasurer and ultimately the Hon. Auditor of the association. He was the moving spirit behind the association's collection of 'lantern slides'.

Steer's beautifully composed photographs are a delight to the eye, as well as providing a valuable record of the past.

Edward Steer died at Sea Point on 17 May 1944, having retained his interest in photography and astronomy throughout his life. Among the movable property listed in his estate were an astronomical telescope, a microscope and a micrographic camera and accessories.

Shortly after his death, his widow donated his fine collection of negatives to the Archives in Cape Town.

THOMAS DANIEL RAVENSCROFT was born at Swellendam on 1 May 1851. His interest in photography dates from his employment by a Cape Town photographer, in 1869.

He travelled widely throughout the Cape Province as an unofficial agent for the Cape Government Railways in the late 1800s, photographing the towns and villages served by the railway. He captured on film almost every aspect of the places he visited: the main streets and important buildings such as churches, schools, post offices, railway stations, and local industries. In most cases, he also took a panoramic view of the town from some elevated spot nearby. Many of these photographs were used by the railway as publicity material, and were the first photographs to be placed in railway carriages for the enjoyment of travellers. Ravenscroft also produced portraits of well-known figures such as Cecil John Rhodes and Sir Henry Bartle Frere.

His work, particularly that of his most prolific period, from 1890 to 1909, is of immense historical importance, and was later described as a 'pictorial history of each town, village or city he visited'.

After living in Cape Town for many years, Ravenscroft retired to Hermanus. Dr EG Malherbe told how Ravenscroft was once photographing him, Jan Hofmeyr and some others, with the 'blowhole' at Hermanus as a backdrop, standing on a promontory with his back to the sea. Ravenscroft was waiting for the water to be forced upwards through the 'blowhole' when a swell came up behind him. He would have been swept out to sea had not some of the group dashed forward to his rescue. However, nothing could save his expensive camera, and Ravenscroft, who was not a rich man, was very upset by its loss.

In late 1944 Ravenscroft (still actively taking photographs at the age of 93) offered for sale his collection of negatives and two large albums of prints. Kathleen Jeffreys of the Archives travelled to Hermanus to evaluate the collection and subsequently recommended that he be offered £190 for the negatives and £10 for the albums. Ravenscroft accepted the offer, and by February 1945 the Ravenscroft Collection, as it is now known, had arrived at the Archives.

Ravenscroft died at Hermanus a few years later, on 24 March 1948. An inventory lists photographic equipment and a portable studio, together valued at £100, among the assets in his estate.

KATHLEEN JEFFREYS was born in Cape Town on 23 August 1893. After completing her schooling, she qualified as a primary school teacher and taught in the Free State for a few years before studying for a Bachelor of Arts and later for a Master of Arts degree.

She joined the Archives in Cape Town in 1919, and remained there for 29 years, until her retirement in 1948. She edited the seven volumes of *Kaapse Archiefstukken*, perhaps her greatest achievement. After retirement she ran the Africana Room at Maskew Miller Ltd, and later set up her own business as a dealer in Africana.

An enthusiastic traveller in her younger days, she spent time in Europe and India. As well as English and Afrikaans, she spoke German, French and Dutch, and even a little Hindustani. She began collecting Africana as a young woman, and over the years amassed a wide variety of books, pamphlets and photographs. Her will (dated 1938) bequeathed this valuable collection to the Archives in Cape Town.

Jeffreys died on 6 July 1968. GC Hamilton Ross, in an obituary in the *Cape Times*, described her as being 'as genuine as the Africana she collected'.

The original entrance to the prison now leads to the Western Cape Archives and Records Service building.

FROM JAIL TO ARCHIVES

WORK BEGAN ON THE NEW JAIL IN ROELAND STREET IN 1856. Its exterior was designed in an ornamental style which the Governor, Sir George Grey, believed would 'have an influence, by no means to be neglected, on the taste of the inhabitants and encourage improvements in the erections of private edifices'.

Shortly afterwards, it was decided that it would be preferable to build a prison nearer the harbour, and work was abandoned. Roeland Street jail was finally completed towards the end of 1859, and the Colonial Engineer, George Pilkington, informed the Governor in a letter that most of the original design had been completed as intended, and that the total cost (including the ornamental work and the steps) was just under £15 000.

A reporter from the *Cape Argus* toured the prison at the end of 1884 and described it as 'quite a palace', whereas the former jail had been 'of the kennel order'. The kitchen, he stated, was able to produce both 'soup of superlative excellence' and 'rice water of homeopathic weakness'.

The prison closed in 1977 when the last prisoners were transferred to Pollsmoor Prison in Tokai. The Secretary of Public Works had announced two years earlier that the prison building would be demolished after closure. Later it was decided to preserve the prison façade and part of the outer wall, and to erect a new, purpose-built building to house the Western Cape Archives and Records Service.

The Archives traces its beginnings to 1876, when a commission was appointed to collect and classify the archives of the Cape Colony. The collection was housed in the basement of the new Parliament buildings from 1886, later moving to a building in Queen Victoria Street, formerly the home of the University of the Cape of Good Hope.

In 1990 the Archives moved to the new building at Roeland Street. In this repository are the earliest documents created in South Africa. The archives of the Council of Policy, the highest authority of the Dutch East India Company, for example, contain the earliest resolutions of this body, passed on the ship *Dromedaris* on 30 December 1651.

Collections include various public and non-public records, as well as maps and books. There are also extensive photograph collections, from which the photographs for this book were chosen.

Aerial view of the Cape Archives Depot, 1989

Roeland Street Prison entrance, 1977

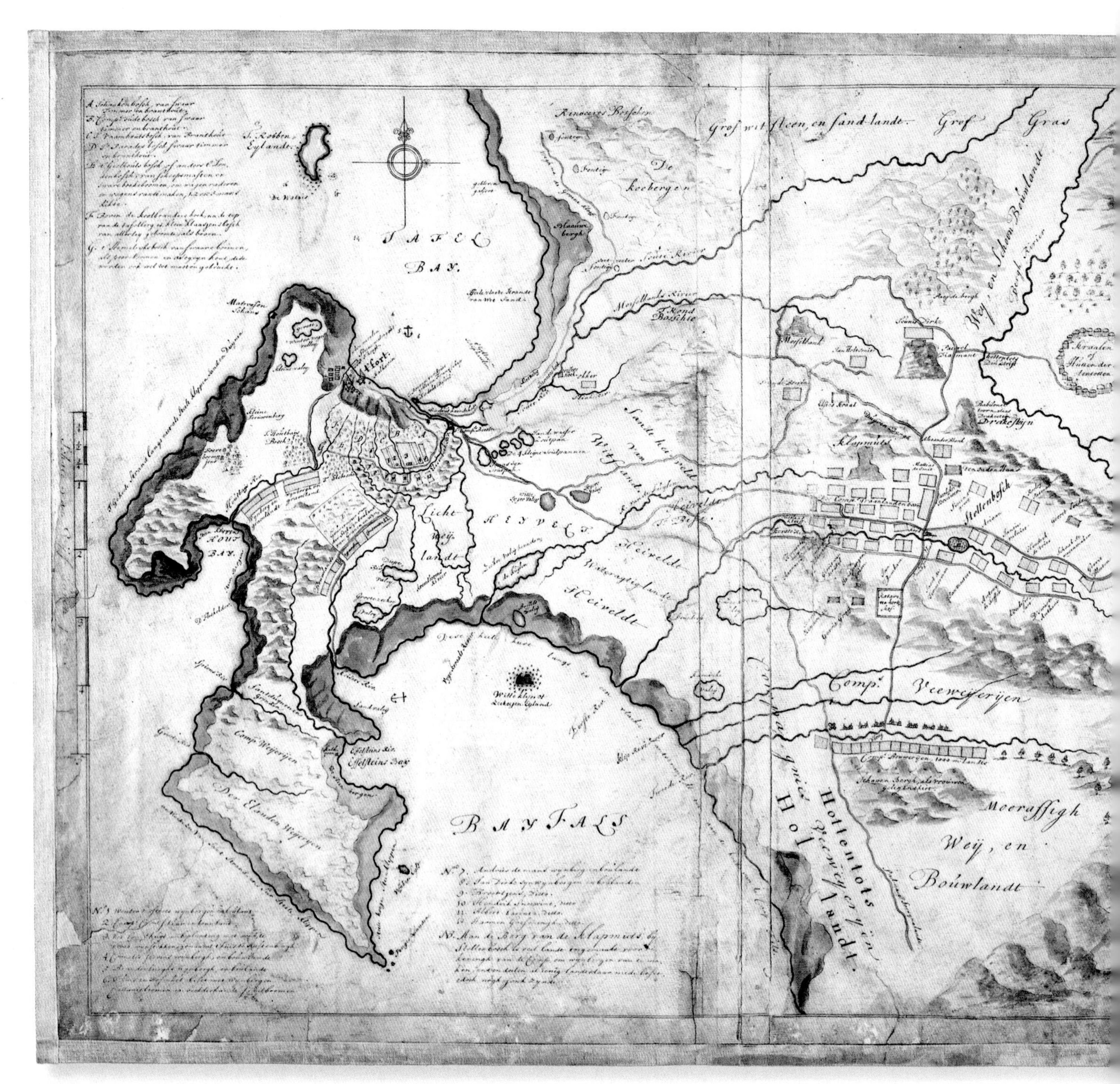

The Cape Peninsula in the eighteenth century (Western Cape Archives and Records Service, M1/273)

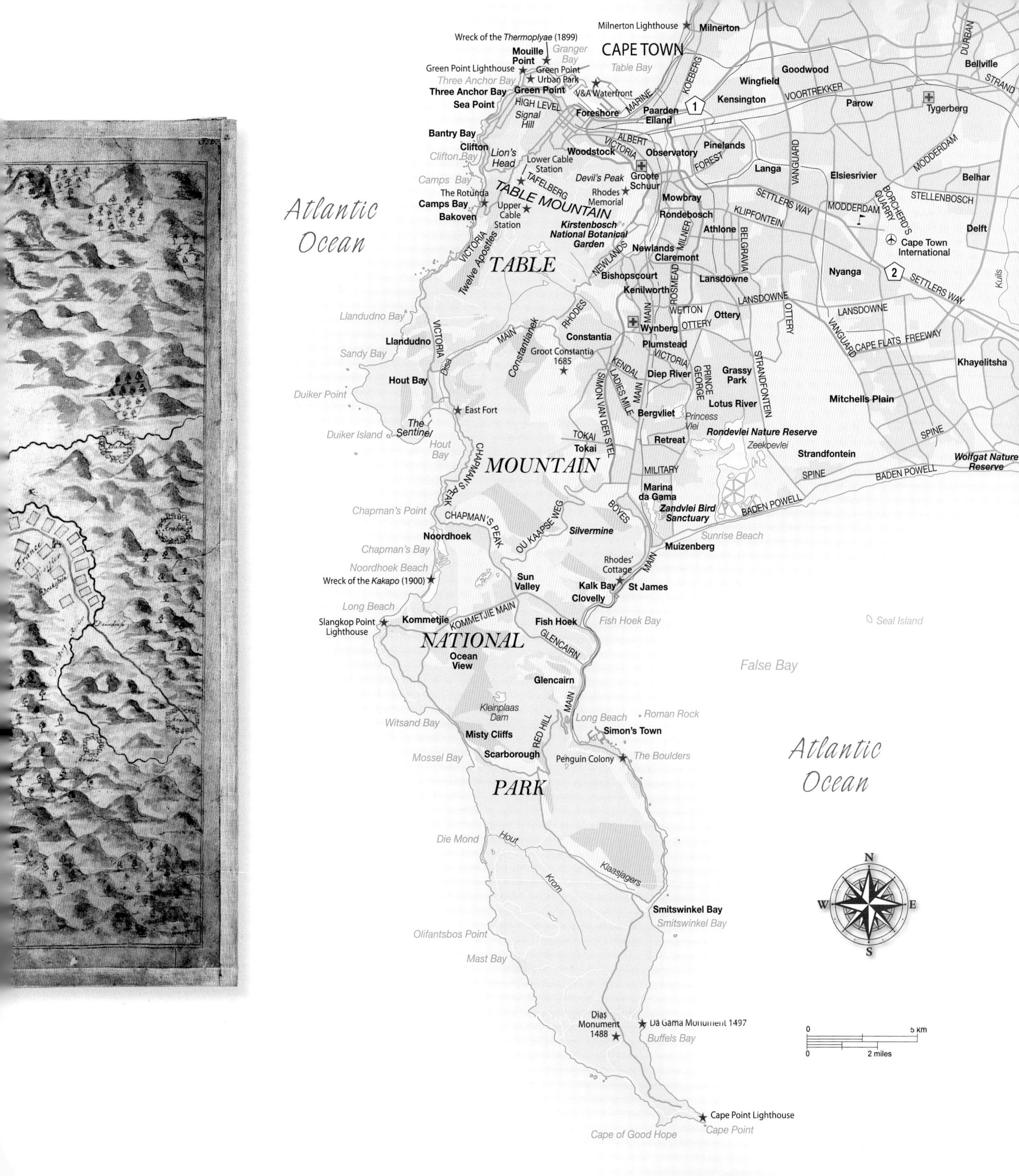

Milnerton Lighthouse
Milnerton
Wreck of the Thermoplyae (1899)
Mouille Point
Granger Bay
CAPE TOWN
Table Bay
Green Point Lighthouse
Green Point Urban Park
Three Anchor Bay
Three Anchor Bay
Green Point
V&A Waterfront
MARINE
KOEBERG
1
Sea Point
HIGH LEVEL
Signal Hill
Foreshore
Paarden Eiland
Goodwood
Wingfield
Kensington
VOORTREKKER
Parow
Tygerberg
Bellville
DURBAN
STRAND
Bantry Bay
Clifton
Clifton Bay
Lion's Head
Lower Cable Station
Woodstock
ALBERT
VICTORIA
Observatory
Pinelands
FOREST
VANGUARD
Langa
Elsiesrivier
MODDERDAM
Belhar
Camps Bay
The Rotunda
Camps Bay
Bakoven
TAFELBERG
TABLE MOUNTAIN
Upper Cable Station
Devil's Peak
Rhodes Memorial
Groote Schuur
Mowbray
Rondebosch
SETTLERS WAY
KLIPFONTEIN
MODDERDAM
BORCHERD'S QUARRY
STELLENBOSCH
Atlantic Ocean
Kirstenbosch National Botanical Garden
VICTORIA
Twelve Apostles
TABLE
NEWLANDS
Newlands
Claremont
MILNER
Athlone
BELGRAVIA
Cape Town International
Delft
Bishopscourt
Kenilworth
ROSMEAD
Lansdowne
Nyanga
2
SETTLERS WAY
Kuils
Llandudno Bay
RHODES
WETTON
LANSDOWNE
Ottery
LANSDOWNE
Llandudno
VICTORIA
MAIN
Constantiaнek
Constantia
MAIN
Wynberg
OTTERY
OTTERY
VANGUARD
CAPE FLATS FREEWAY
Sandy Bay
Groot Constantia 1685
Plumstead
VICTORIA
KENDAL
Diep River
PRINCE GEORGE
Grassy Park
STRANDFONTEIN
Khayelitsha
Hout Bay
Disa
SIMON VAN DER STEL
LADIES MILE
MAIN
Lotus River
Mitchells Plain
Duiker Point
East Fort
Bergvliet
Princess Vlei
The Sentinel
Duiker Island
Hout Bay
CHAPMAN'S PEAK
TOKAI
Tokai
Retreat
Rondevlei Nature Reserve
Zeekoevlei
SPINE
Strandfontein
Wolfgat Nature Reserve
MOUNTAIN
MILITARY
SPINE
BADEN POWELL
Marina da Gama
Chapman's Point
CHAPMAN'S PEAK
OU KAAPSE WEG
BOYES
Zandvlei Bird Sanctuary
BADEN POWELL
Silvermine
Sunrise Beach
Noordhoek
Chapman's Bay
Muizenberg
Noordhoek Beach
Rhodes' Cottage
MAIN
Wreck of the Kakapo (1900)
Sun Valley
Kalk Bay
St James
Clovelly
Long Beach
Slangkop Point Lighthouse
Kommetjie
KOMMETJIE MAIN
Fish Hoek
Fish Hoek Bay
Seal Island
NATIONAL
GLENCAIRN
Ocean View
False Bay
Glencairn
Kleinplaas Dam
MAIN
Long Beach
Roman Rock
Witsand Bay
RED HILL
Simon's Town
Misty Cliffs
Scarborough
Penguin Colony
The Boulders
Mossel Bay
Atlantic Ocean
PARK
Die Mond
Hout
Klaasjagers
Krom
N
W
E
S
Smitswinkel Bay
Smitswinkel Bay
Olifantsbos Point
Mast Bay
Dias Monument 1488
Da Gama Monument 1497
Buffels Bay
0
5 km
0
2 miles
Cape Point Lighthouse
Cape of Good Hope
Cape Point

For many years, fishing boats used to beach at Roggebaai to unload their catch. In the late 1930s, plans were made to develop and upgrade Cape Town harbour. A new quay, parallel to a long mole, was planned. Work began in 1937 and millions of cubic metres of mud and sand were dredged from the basin between the quay and the mole to create what is now the Foreshore and the Duncan and Ben Schoeman docks.

Table Mountain is instantly recognised across the world and forms an impressive backdrop to the city. It is part of a sandstone mountain range extending across the Cape Peninsula, and its main feature is the plateau, flanked by Lion's Head to the west and by Devil's Peak to the east.

The vegetation on the mountain consists of Cape fynbos, and over 2 000 species of plants found here are unique to this location. The dassie (or rock hyrax) is the most common mammal, but Table Mountain is also home to tortoise, porcupine and various snake species.

The top of the mountain is frequently covered by a 'tablecloth' of cloud. This is caused when a southeasterly wind is directed up the slopes to meet colder air, where the moisture condenses to form a cloud.

The first recorded ascent of Table Mountain was made in 1503 by António de Saldanha, a Portuguese explorer, who named it Taboa do Cabo ('Table of

the Cape'). Lady Anne Barnard (wife of Andrew Barnard, Secretary to the Cape administration) climbed the mountain in 1797, accompanied by three gentlemen, several slaves and her personal maid. Two centuries later General Jan Christiaan Smuts (the second Prime Minister of South Africa) regularly made the climb from his residence at Groote Schuur.

In 1926 the construction of a cableway to give easy access to the summit was proposed. This project was completed at a cost of £60 000, and the official opening took place on 4 October 1929. The first cars carried 19 passengers and a conductor. The present two cars, installed in a major upgrade in 1997, can carry 65 people and boast revolving floors which allow passengers to enjoy views through 360 degrees.

In 2012, Table Mountain was voted one of the New7Wonders of Nature, and a bronze plaque to this effect was unveiled on 2 December 2012 at the boardwalk near the lower cable station.

Table Bay was first named Saldanha Bay, after the Portuguese explorer António de Saldanha, who anchored there in 1503. In 1601, the commander of a Dutch fleet anchored in the bay renamed it Table Bay.

The bay became a popular revictualling point for ships after the Dutch settlement was established in 1652. However, the bay had serious deficiencies as an anchorage, and many ships at anchor in Table Bay were wrecked during winter storms over the next two hundred years. This problem was only solved by the harbour works of the 1860s. These photographs show how Table Bay and the city of Cape Town have altered over the past hundred or so years.

The Castle of Good Hope is the oldest building in South Africa. The cornerstones for the building were laid in 1665. Built in the shape of a pentagon, with a bastion at each corner, it was first occupied in 1674.

The five bastions were named after the titles held by the Prince of Orange: Buren (north), Leerdam (west), Katzenellenbogen (east), Nassau (northwest) and Oranje (southwest). The original entrance was between Katzenellenbogen and Buren, and faced the sea, which at that time reached the castle walls. In 1682 a new gateway, which is the present entrance, was built. A 25-metre-wide moat was dug around the Castle to offer further protection.

Inside the massive walls was the Governor's residence, fronted by the imposing De Kat balcony. Here the new Governor was sworn in and proclamations were made. Also within the Castle were quarters for officers and men, cells for prisoners, storerooms, workshops and kitchens.

The Castle was extensively renovated in the 1980s. Today it is the best preserved example of a Dutch East India Company fort and a popular tourist attraction, as well as being an active military facility. In the Governor's residence is displayed part of the William Fehr Collection, a noted collection of oil paintings, furniture and decorative items from the colonial period.

The Grand Parade was the first public open space in Cape Town. It was used as the training ground for the Castle garrison. Public functions, such as the annual celebration of Queen Victoria's birthday, were also held here, and there was a regular market.

The Parade became known as the Grand Parade to distinguish it from the Little Parade, later named Caledon Square. Various buildings were constructed around the perimeter: the City Hall, an Opera House, the Drill Hall and the Commercial Exchange.

The City Hall, now the home of the Cape Philharmonic Orchestra, was designed in the Italian Renaissance style and built of Bath stone. This impressive building was

completed in 1905. The clock in the tower was modelled on Big Ben in London, but is half the size. The tower contained 37 bells, first rung when the Prince of Wales visited South Africa in 1925. Later, another two bells were added.

The red-roofed Drill Hall, visible to the left of the City Hall, opened in 1885 and was designed to serve as an indoor venue for military drilling in bad weather and as the headquarters of the Western Division of the armed forces. Today it houses the Cape Town Central Library. The Opera House was demolished in 1937.

The present-day Parade is half its original size. When Cape Town station was built in 1879, it swallowed up part of the Parade. The impressive Victorian station building was demolished in the 1960s and a modern rail terminal erected in its place.

BRASSO LIQUID METAL POLISH
FLAG
5
41

The street now known as Adderley Street has had several changes of name over the years. Initially it was known as Burgwal, then as Voorste Straat. When the canal (*gracht*) was later constructed, it became known as Heerengracht.

Charles Bowyer Adderley was a British politician. In 1849, when the British government announced plans to establish a penal colony at the Cape, he vigorously defended the Cape's refusal to allow this. Thus Heerengracht was renamed Adderley Street as a gesture of gratitude.

Trams and hansom cabs were still to be seen in Adderley Street in the 1920s, but in 1939 the last tram ran and horse-drawn vehicles eventually gave way to motor traffic.

A number of the buildings depicted in photographs taken circa 1910 still exist and are immediately recognisable. Even though some of them have been modernised at ground level, a glance at the upper storeys will confirm their Victorian origins.

The magnificent Standard Bank building in Adderley Street was designed in 1880 by Charles Freeman. Built by Thomas Ingleby, it cost £27 000. Initially the building had only two floors (as can be seen in the photograph on the left), but in 1897 an additional two floors were added. In 1921 further alterations were made, and the statue of Britannia was replaced on the high dome.

The Standard Bank of British South Africa was established in London in 1862. The colonial head office of the bank was initially in Port Elizabeth. (Later, the name was changed to the Standard Bank of South Africa.) Cape Town, having better communications with both the interior of the country and overseas, became the location of the bank's head office in 1885.

This was the headquarters of the bank for 68 years, until the head office moved to Pretoria in 1953. By 2011 it housed less than 100 employees and the decision was taken to close the old building and move all banking activity to the Standard Bank branch in Thibault Square.

NOW OPEN
GRAND NATIONAL BAZAAR AND
& CO LTD
H.W. MARKHAM CLOTHIER
MARKHAM'S
GENTLEMEN'S OUTFITTERS
COMPLETE HOUSEHOLD FURNISHERS
H.W. MARKHAM
MILKMAID MILK
Sold Everywhere
MILKMAID MILK
ORANJEZICHT
14

Adderley Street in 1905, looking towards the harbour. The department store Stuttafords, founded in 1857 by Samuel Rickart Stuttaford, is on the left. Next to it is Markhams, a men's outfitters, founded in 1873.

GARLICK'S
WHOLESALE

THE PIER

THE MUNICIPALITY OF CAPE TOWN'S NEW PIER was completed in 1913 at a cost of £85 000. The lower level offered rowing boats for hire, a platform for anglers and bathing boxes. On the upper levels were a restaurant, a concert hall and a bandstand.

A promenade on the pier became fashionable, and people flocked to the free concerts. As late as the 1930s, entrance to the pier cost only one penny.

Sadly, though, the pier was demolished after the Second World War, when it was decided to reclaim 65 hectares of land in Roggebaai from the sea.

The municipal pier was built close to the spot where Jan van Riebeeck was thought to have landed on 6 April 1652. Van Riebeeck had been sent to the Cape by the Dutch East India Company (Vereenigde Oost-Indische Compagnie, or VOC) to establish a station where Company ships could revictual on the voyage to and from the East Indies. This was the first European settlement in southern Africa.

Cape premier and mining magnate Cecil John Rhodes commissioned a statue of Jan van Riebeeck, to be placed at the foot of Adderley Street, at the spot where he landed in 1652. The bronze statue, sculpted by John Tweed, was unveiled on 18 May 1899. A nearby statue of Van Riebeeck's wife, Maria, was erected in 1952, a gift of the Dutch government.

At the time, the statue of Van Riebeeck stood almost at the water's edge, and can be seen here adjacent to the pier (above and right). Nowadays, as a result of the reclamation of the Foreshore, the statue, still on the same spot, is marooned on a traffic island (inset photo), almost a kilometre from the sea.

DOGS ARE
STRICTLY

Work began on the first Cape Town harbour in 1860. Prince Alfred, the second son of Queen Victoria, inaugurated the harbour works by tipping the first load of stone for the new breakwater on 17 September.

Work suffered a setback in 1865, when the 'Great Gale' hit Cape Town on 17 May. Eighteen ships were wrecked and number of lives lost. In addition, a section of the newly built breakwater was damaged. But this storm made it perfectly clear that a breakwater and properly sheltered anchorage were essential.

The new inner and outer basins within the new breakwater were officially opened by Prince Alfred, on his second visit to the Cape in 1870, and named the Alfred Dock.

It soon became obvious that the harbour was not large enough to accommodate the increasing number of vessels arriving at the Cape. In 1889 work began on a new outer basin, which was named the Victoria Basin. Further extensions followed as traffic increased and ships became larger.

Horse-drawn drays remained the main means of transporting goods in nineteenth-century Cape Town, although the railway between Cape Town station and the docks opened in 1875. In the middle distance at left is the clock tower, and at right is a forest of masts of ships moored in the Alfred Basin, against the backdrop of Table Mountain.

From the earliest days, Cape Town was nicknamed 'Tavern of the Seas', and has always welcomed ships and sailors making the long voyage round the southern tip of Africa. The image on this page, from the early 1900s, shows a visiting Argentine naval training ship. In the early days, the only vessels in the harbour would have been sailing ships. Eventually sail gave way to steam power, but the harbour has remained a vital part of the local economy.

Nowadays, although the normal business of the harbour continues, mainly in the form of container handling, fishing and marine repairs, there is an additional emphasis on leisure activities. Various companies offer daily sailing and motor cruises from the V&A Waterfront, and there are regular tourist ferries to Robben Island. International cruise ships make regular stops in Cape Town. It is even possible to take a helicopter tour from the harbour.

NELSON MANDELA GATEWAY
CLOCK TOWER

The Victorian clock tower was initially used as the Port Captain's office. On the lowest level is a mechanism that was used to check tide levels. On the second floor is a room from which the Port Captain could keep an eye on harbour activities. At the top of the building is the clock mechanism.

The Clock Tower was restored in 1997 and is a prominent feature of the V&A Waterfront, named after Queen Victoria and her son Alfred. The photo above shows the Nelson Mandela Gateway, the new terminal for ferries to and from Robben Island.

The project to develop the Waterfront was launched in the late 1980s, and the complex is today the most-visited attraction in Cape Town. There are shopping centres, restaurants of every description, tourist attractions (such as the Two Oceans Aquarium), museums (such as the Maritime Centre and SAS *Somerset*) and luxury hotels.

Part of the appeal of the V&A Waterfront is that this modern development has been integrated with the working commercial harbour.

The view across the city centre from Signal Hill has altered dramatically over the years. In 1890, when this photo was taken, flat-roofed buildings of one or two storeys predominated, the view punctuated here and there by church spires or the towers of public buildings. Just over a hundred years later, high-rise office blocks dominate the scene (left).

YE OLD THATCHED TAVERN

Greenmarket Square, as the name suggests, was the site of Cape Town's fruit and vegetable market. It is the second oldest public space in Cape Town (the Grand Parade being the oldest). A burgher watch house was built there in 1696, from which the watchmen would patrol the streets at night.

The Old Town House, completed in 1761, was built on the site of the old watch house and served as the Burgher Senate and the city hall. It is now a museum housing the Michaelis Collection of early Dutch and Flemish art.

Various businesses had premises on Greenmarket Square. The oldest hotel in Cape Town, Ye Old Thatched Tavern (which lost its thatch in the early nineteenth century), was situated next to the Old Town House.

Opposite the Old Town House is the Metropolitan Methodist Church. The development of Methodism at the Cape owes much to the Reverend Barnabas Shaw, who arrived here in 1816. Shaw was largely instrumental in the erection of the first Wesleyan Methodist church in Cape Town, on the corner of Burg and Church streets, in 1829. By the 1870s this church was too small. The plot on which the present church stands was bought for £1 850 in 1875, and building commenced in 1878. The architect was Charles Freeman, who designed the Standard Bank building in Adderley Street. The first service was held in November 1879.

For a number of years the square was used as a car park. Subsequently it became a marketplace once again, and is now a popular craft and curio market.

IRONMONCERY WAREHOUSE
PROTECT

There were a number of businesses in Greenmarket Square by the 1880s. The Cape of Good Hope Almanac *for 1881 lists a snuff manufacturer, a cabinetmaker, a watchmaker, a jeweller, import agents and commission agents, as well as the Singer Sewing Machine Company (clearly visible in this photograph).*

By the early 1890s, boarding houses and eating places had been opened. Mrs E Thorne's private boarding house, Jeremiah Murphy's restaurant, and a Temperance Restaurant were all situated on the square.

STRAND STREET
COFFEE
NEWS AGENTS AND STATIONERS
35
MEALS

Strand Street, first known as Zeestraat ('sea street'), was originally only a short distance from the sea. (The reclamation of the Foreshore placed it about a kilometre inland.) This was where many wealthy merchants built substantial homes. An example is the Koopmans-de Wet House, which is now a museum.

At the turn of the twentieth century, a number of businesses were situated in Strand Street, such as the stationer's shop and 'coffee palace' visible in the photograph on the left. Since then, some of the buildings have been replaced by a parking lot and an intersection.

The main image shows the Canadian Field Artillery proceeding up Strand Street, probably on their way to the camp on Green Point Common, during the Second Anglo-Boer War (1899–1902). More than 28 000 volunteers from Canada, New Zealand and Australia took part in the war, as well as over 365 000 British troops. Altogether some 22 000 men died. A large number of these casualties were as a result of wounds or disease, and only a relative minority were killed in action.

The colourful Bo-Kaap area (formerly referred to as the 'Malay Quarter') presents another side of central Cape Town. The narrow streets are steep, still cobbled in places, and the semi-detached houses, most painted in vibrant colours, are plain in design.

Many of the present-day inhabitants of the Bo-Kaap are descendants of slaves brought to the Cape by the Dutch East India Company from Batavia (Java), Ceylon, Malaya and India. The majority of these were Muslims.

Chiappini Street forms the boundary of the old 'Malay Quarter' and in many ways epitomises the spirit of the Bo-Kaap. There are two mosques in this street: the Jamia Mosque (established in 1850) and the Mosque Shafee (established in 1859). The original Mosque Shafee (shown in the old photograph) collapsed in the 1940s, but a new mosque was erected on the same site (shown in the photograph above).

Bo-Kaap homes clustered on the lower slopes of Signal Hill to the right of Rose Street provide lively splashes of colour. In the background is Lion's Head.

CAPE TOWN PAINT DEPOT
PAINT DEPOT
POINT
BUILDING
SUPPLIES

A gentleman climber surveys the view from his rather precarious seat at Kloof Corner on Table Mountain. In the background are Lion's Head and Signal Hill, with Robben Island a smudge in the distance. The vista today is considerably more urbanised.

In the eighteenth century, Green Point Common was known as 'De Waterplaats' and stretched from Three Anchor Bay to Cape Town. The extent of the Common has been much reduced over the years as parts have been taken over for various purposes. In 1860 Fort Wynyard was built on the site of an old Dutch East India Company battery. Somerset Hospital, the first teaching hospital in South Africa, was opened in 1864.

The first horse race at the Cape was held on Green Point Common in 1797, and the Common continued to be used as a racecourse until 1890. Some of the earliest cricket and rugby matches were played here, and sports fields are still a feature of the Common today. A golf course was laid out, and the Green Point track catered for cycling and track sports.

During the Second Anglo-Boer War (1899–1902), the Common was turned into an army camp, with orderly rows of huts and tents to accommodate some

of the tens of thousands of troops who poured into the country. A prisoner-of-war camp was also situated here, from which about 26 000 Boer prisoners were shipped to camps in distant St Helena, Bermuda, Ceylon and India.

The Common is now dominated by the oval Cape Town Stadium, which was constructed at a cost of R4.4 billion for the 2010 FIFA World Cup™. Construction began in March 2007, and was completed within 33 months. The 64 000-seat stadium (the capacity was reduced to 55 000 after the World Cup) replaced the old 18 000-seat Green Point Stadium, which was used mainly for soccer matches and music concerts. The building of the stadium was accompanied by a general revamp of the Common, including construction of the multipurpose Green Point Urban Park.

Cape Town Stadium is operated by the City of Cape Town, and the venue caters for soccer matches (both club-level and international), concerts and other major events. There are also training and conference facilities available.

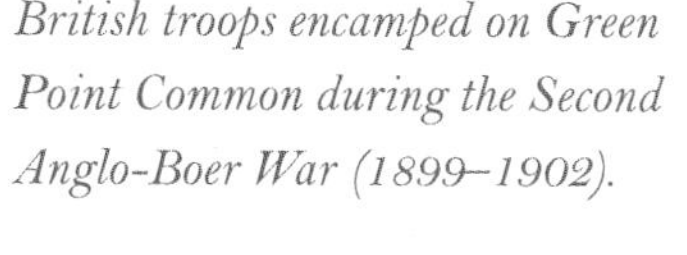

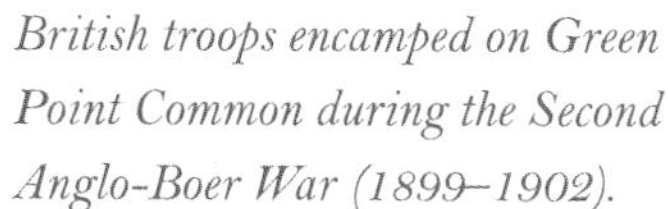

British troops encamped on Green Point Common during the Second Anglo-Boer War (1899–1902).

OVERLEAF: A panoramic view takes in the sweep of Cape Town's Atlantic seaboard, from the V&A Waterfront at left, past Cape Town Stadium, Green Point, Mouille Point and round to Sea Point and Bantry Bay at far right. Above the city rises the bulk of Signal Hill and Lion's Head, with the Table Mountain massif in the background.

The lighthouse on Beach Road, Mouille Point, is commonly known as the Mouille Point lighthouse but is in fact the Green Point lighthouse, completed in 1824. Its popular name derives from a structure built near Granger Bay and later demolished. Green Point is the oldest lighthouse still in operation in South Africa, and is a well-known local landmark.

A government notice was published on 9 April 1824 stating that 'the Light House, erected on the projecting Point of Land between the Great Mouillêe, or Moulin Battery, and Three Anchor Bay, under the Lion's Rump, at the entrance of Table Bay, being now completed, the Lighting thereof will commence on Monday, the 12th instant'.

The name Mouille Point comes from the Dutch word *moilje* ('breakwater'), and refers to the unsuccessful attempts, begun in 1743, to construct a mole to protect ships anchored in Table Bay. Later, in 1781, when France and Holland were at war with Britain, French troops stationed at the battery next to the abandoned mole referred to the Mouille Battery, and it is this version of the name which has survived.

In common with the rest of the Atlantic seaboard of Cape Town, the dusty, unsurfaced road and unpretentious houses have given way to a tarred road flanked by high-rise apartment buildings. The nearby seafront promenade is a popular spot for walkers, runners and dog-walkers.

SS THERMOPYLAE

ON MONDAY 11 SEPTEMBER 1899, THE *THERMOPYLAE*, a steamship of the Aberdeen White Star Company under the command of Captain Philip, approached Cape Town. It was a misty night with a fine drizzle. As well as 52 passengers and a crew of 84 men, the ship carried 20 boxes of specie (valued at £100 000) and two valuable racehorses. One of these was the property of Mrs De Barthe (better known as Lillie Langtry, a celebrated actress and at one time the mistress of the future King Edward VII).

Captain Philip was misled by the mist into believing that he was further from the shore than he was. Too late he recognised the danger, and the ship struck the Mouille Point reef.

All the passengers and crew were safely landed, but the horses were left in their horse-boxes forward of the bridge. By the early hours of Tuesday morning a heavy sea was running, with waves breaking over the ship. Fortunately, the horses were eventually brought safely to land. The valuable cargo of specie was also saved.

A board of enquiry found that the loss of the ship was due to the captain's error of judgement, and his master's certificate was suspended for six months.

Although the photograph above shows the area where the *Thermopylae* ran aground, the wreckage visible in the picture is in all probability the rusted boiler machinery belonging to the RMS *Athens*, a steam-driven mailship of 739 tons, which was driven ashore much earlier, in fact – during the Great Gale of 17 May 1865.

The name Three Anchor Bay was first recorded in 1661 and is supposed to refer to a defensive chain, held in place by three anchors, across the entrance to the small anchorage.

In the nineteenth century, a number of people applied to the colonial government for permission to establish business ventures at Three Anchor Bay. In 1807 Cornelis Moll wished to establish a lime-burning business 'in the vicinity of the sea strand betwixt the so called Three Ancres Bay and the Society's House at the westward of the Lion's Rump'.

A year later Jan Tenius asked for a grant of three acres of ground 'between Cape Town and the Society House … in the proximity of the Moulie and the usually so called Drie Anker' in order to establish a vegetable garden. Neither of these gentlemen obtained the permission he sought.

In 1813 Messrs Melville and De Necker were 'desirous of adventuring on the Establishment of a Fishery for the Catching and Curing (by salting and drying in the Sun) of Cray-fish', which they intended to sell to Mauritius and Réunion as well as to sailors from the East. Unfortunately there is no record of whether the application was successful.

The *Cape of Good Hope Almanac* of 1881 lists nine private residents in Three Anchor Bay, all of them businessmen working in Cape Town, as well as a boarding house run by a Mrs De Jongh. The scene is quite different today.

In 1889 Sea Point began to develop as a residential suburb of Cape Town. The privately owned railway between Cape Town and Sea Point was taken over by the Cape Government Railways in 1905, but could not compete with the service offered by the Electric Tramway Company. Although this was the first line in South Africa to be electrified, the fact that it was uneconomic led to the closure of the line in 1929.

The tranquil life of Sea Point in the early 1900s has changed considerably. Blocks of flats line the beachfront, and the area is one of the most densely populated in the Peninsula.

The Sea Point promenade, a paved walkway that hugs the sea front for six kilometres, follows part of the former railway permanent way. Popular with walkers and runners, the promenade offers excellent sea views and often captivating sunsets.

The Queen's Hotel, a popular base for seaside holidays, stood near the shore at Saunders Rocks. The first building on this site dated from 1767 and was a recreation centre known as the Societeits Huis ('Society House'). By 1800 it was a private home. In 1835, under the ownership of Mr Justice William Menzies, it was considerably enlarged and became known as Sea Point House.

Sea Point House first became a hotel in 1876. Initially known as the Sea Point Hotel, it was later renamed the Wenthworth Hotel. In 1887 the old structure was demolished, and an elegant building erected in its place. This was named the Queen's Hotel in honour of Queen Victoria's Golden Jubilee.

The hotel was built (1882–1889) by Thomas James Ingleby, who started up as a builder on his own account in 1851. He was responsible for a number of buildings in Cape Town, including the new post office building (1874) and the Standard Bank building in Adderley Street (1882).

An advertisement for the hotel in 1909 stated that it had 'a large private garden, electric light and all modern improvements'. Cape Town was only a 15-minute journey away by railway or electric tram.

In the early 1900s, Sea Point was a place of gracious and elegant residences. Just over a century later, the suburb is heavily built up and has expanded up the mountainside.

Bantry Bay was originally known as Botany Bay. A botanical garden was established here in the early 1800s by Dr Friedrich Ludwig Liesching (later the first president of the South African Medical Society), mainly for growing medicinal herbs. The garden was abandoned after a few years, but the name Botany Bay remained in use until the land was purchased by a Mr O'Callaghan. He renamed it Bantry Bay after the well-known inlet on the southwestern coast of Ireland.

This was one of the most attractive and unspoilt areas of the Cape Peninsula. After the First World War, a number of British families settled at the Cape, one of whom was Captain LG Fenner. He bought a tract of land at Bantry Bay and built a block of flats, which he named Bantry Court Flats. (The concept of living in a flat was relatively unknown in the Peninsula at the time.)

This was the first step in the development of Bantry Bay, and by the 1950s almost all the slopes overlooking the bay had been built over, and its charm had been lost. Today the coast is lined with apartment blocks, and there is virtually no access to the shore.

Clifton, with the tramway route visible above the coast road, was originally known as Schoenmakersgat ('cobbler's hole' in Dutch), supposedly because a shoemaker lived in one of the caves in that area. The first official reference to the name was in 1802, when the Acting Governor of the Cape directed that 'a small piece of Ground facing the sea under the Lion's Head called Schoenmakers Gat' be registered in the name of a Major McNab, who was to pay an annual rent of 24 rix-dollars.

The property was sold to Henry Hewitt, a merchant, circa 1829, and the house that stood here was renamed Kloof Cottage. Eventually it became a hotel. In the early 1890s a Mrs Bess Clifton was manager of the hotel, and it is likely that this is the origin of the later name Clifton-on-Sea.

Today Clifton is one of the most exclusive addresses in Cape Town, and properties change hands for many millions of rands.

CLIFTON ON SEA HOTEL

There are four beaches at Clifton, separated by falls of large granite boulders. The granite sand is dazzlingly white. These beaches are one of the few areas that are sheltered from the southeasterly wind, and this has added to their popularity. In this photograph, the Clifton-on-Sea Hotel is clearly visible on the coast road, above the rocky shore.

The Clifton-on-Sea Hotel is described by the *Cape Town Guide* of 1900 as 'charmingly situated' and 'far from the noise, dust and wind of the city'. In 1905 Clifton was described in the *Handbook of Cape Town and Suburbs* as 'a small group of houses just above the road, with cultivated grounds extending down the hillside towards the Clifton-on-Sea hotel – a solitary landmark on the Victoria Road'.

By 1913, Clifton was a popular camping spot, and in his book *Our Beautiful Peninsula* Herbert Tucker vividly describes the scene: 'The quaint many-coloured wigwams of quite a considerable community of campers' were clustered on the 'steep and broken shoreward slopes' of Clifton Bay. The camp sites were leased

to summer residents, and later the lessees built bungalows on the sites, although they were not allowed to live there permanently, being required to vacate their properties in the winter. This restriction was only lifted in 1929.

In 1950 the *Guide to South and Eastern Africa* described Clifton-on-Sea as 'a pretty resort' with good rock fishing, although it warned that 'bathing [was] dangerous, except in certain localities'.

Nowadays the slopes above and below Victoria Road are crowded with ultra-luxurious homes and apartment complexes – a far cry from the modest wooden bungalows of the early twentieth century.

This view of Camps Bay, with the Rotunda visible on the left, shows one of the trams that ran between Cape Town and Camps Bay. The first electric trams ran in 1896. Five years later, on 9 May 1901, the line between Cape Town and Camps Bay (via Sea Point) was opened, and this initiated the transformation of Camps Bay into a popular holiday resort. The single-decker tramcars were painted in an elegant cream and chocolate livery.

In 1902, a further section of tramway was built from the terminus at Camps Bay, over Kloof Nek, to Cape Town. The 19-kilometre trip 'around the mountain' became a popular excursion. Travelling time along this route was an hour and a quarter, and cost one shilling and nine pence.

A guide to Cape Town published in 1904 described the tram ride from Cape Town to Camps Bay as 'without doubt the most beautiful in the world, affording one vast panorama of matchless beauty'.

The Rotunda was built in 1904, and was the brainchild of James Riddell Farquhar, whose aim was to promote Camps Bay as a holiday resort. All kinds of events took place here, including concerts, dances, silent film shows and boxing matches.

A new section was added to the Rotunda in the 1950s. Subsequently, when new owners decided to demolish the building and put up a seven-storey block of flats, a storm of protest by Camps Bay residents led to the Rotunda being declared a heritage site.

This photograph shows the tram route from Kloof Nek to Camps Bay, below the rocky buttresses of the Twelve Apostles. It was only in the 1930s that this route became a public road. It is now known as Camps Bay Drive. Near the shore is the chimney of the tramway power station and depot, with the Rotunda clearly visible nearby.

With its serried ranks of palm trees and upmarket shops and restaurants, Victoria Road is virtually unrecognisable from the days when cattle ambled beside the quiet coastal road.

Camps Bay's wide sandy beach makes it one of Cape Town's most popular seaside escapes, while the tiny village of yesteryear has mushroomed into a major city suburb. The Rotunda, visible in the foreground, is now part of a luxury hotel complex and is a sought-after venue for functions such as conferences and weddings.

This view of Llandudno, circa 1893, was taken from Victoria Road. Llandudno is situated in a valley facing the Atlantic Ocean, with Twelve Apostles on one side and the Karbonkelberg ('Carbuncle Mountain') on the other. For centuries this area, known as Kleinkommetjie Bay, was inhabited by the Khoisan. A track, along which the Khoisan drove the cattle they bartered to the Dutch, ran from this wilderness to the settlement that became Cape Town. It was only in the 1880s that a proper road was built, when Thomas Bain constructed a coastal road between Camps Bay and Hout Bay. The road, opened shortly before Queen Victoria's Golden Jubilee in 1887, was named in her honour.

In 1903 the area was declared a township. A Mrs Wege, who had recently made a trip to Britain, noticed that Kleinkommetjie Bay looked remarkably similar to the bay at Llandudno, a popular seaside resort in Wales. So it came about that the nascent village was named Llandudno.

The first house was built in 1905, but by 1930 there were still only two permanent residents. People came to Llandudno at weekends, many of them camping in the caves among the boulders in the small cove adjacent to the attractive white beach. Slowly the township grew, with houses being built right up to Victoria Road, but the area has remained unspoilt to this day.

The first visitors to Hout Bay were sailors on the ship *Consent*, which anchored just outside the bay in July 1609. The mate, most probably a man named John Chapman, was sent in a pinnace to judge the bay's suitability as a harbour. The ship's pilot named the bay Chapman's Chance, and described it as a 'very good harboure for ships: for the maine land of the Cape will be shut in upon the wester-side of the land'.

In May 1652, shortly after Jan van Riebeeck's arrival at the Cape, an expedition discovered a fine forest in the area. This became the main source of timber for the Dutch East India Company. The name Hout Bay first appears in Van Riebeeck's journal entry for 11 July 1653, when he referred to it as '*de schone bosschagie … genaemdt de Houtbay*' (the beautiful wooded area named Hout Bay).

The first farmers in the area were Pieter van der Westhuizen and Schalk Willem van der Merwe, who were granted land there in 1677. They were to plant grain, and send 10 per cent of their harvest to the Dutch East India Company. However, trying to wrest a harvest from virgin land was not easy, and the wild animals in the area carried off their cattle. Both farmers gave up the unequal struggle and returned to Table Bay.

Later efforts at farming were more successful, and the farm named Kronendal flourished. When the Kronendal estate was put up for auction in 1832, its extent was about 2 200 morgen (1 880 hectares). The advertisement of the auction in the *Cape Argus* mentions 'a large and commodious dwelling house, wine store, stabling, slave apartments, blacksmith's shop, [and] water mill'

A view of Hout Bay around the turn of the twentieth century showing visitors on an outing to the bay. Note the two Cape carts with canvas hoods, unique to South Africa, which were widely used in the past.

In the background, at left, a natural pedestal of granite can be seen. A statue of a leopard, by local sculptor Ivan Mitford-Barberton, was placed on this rock in 1963 as a memorial to the many wild animals which once flourished in this area.

The East Fort in Hout Bay was one of two batteries constructed in 1781 when the Dutch feared that the British would invade the Cape. The western one was known as Sluysken, and the eastern as Gordon.

The Hout Bay forts saw action briefly when the British took the Cape in 1795. Commodore Blankett reported that he had arrived at Hout Bay on 15 September, and sailed towards the shore, 'the enemy keeping up a smart fire from the two Batteries'.

The Dutch surrendered on 16 September, and all Dutch East India Company assets were handed over to the British. An inventory of these assets includes the following: 'The post in the Hout Bay, with the cultivated Valley as far as the Mattrosen Drift; the Battery Sluysken; the Battery Gordon'.

Both forts fell into ruin in later years, but the East Fort, which housed a powder magazine and an officer's quarters, has been restored as a tourist attraction.

The fishing village on the bay was probably established circa 1867, when a German immigrant named Jacob Trautman settled there. As well as farming, he began a fishing industry, salting fish for export to Mauritius.

Hout Bay remained an isolated but charming little village with almost no economic importance until the 1940s, when it became the centre of a lucrative commercial fishing enterprise. The harbour is still the centre of a tuna and crayfish industry today, and the Hout Bay valley has become a heavily populated residential area.

THE KAKAPO

THE *KAKAPO*, A STEAMSHIP OF 1 093 tons under the command of Captain P Nicholayson, was on her maiden voyage from Swansea, Wales, to Sydney, Australia. When the ship left Cape Town on 25 May 1900 a northwesterly gale was blowing, and in the darkness the captain mistook Chapman's Peak for Cape Point. He steamed full ahead, only to ground his ship on the sands of Noordhoek beach.

At the turn of the century Noordhoek was an isolated spot, with only a few farms in the area. At dawn, the crew of 20 men climbed from the ship onto the sand, and a few of them made their way to one of the farms to report what had happened.

It is said that the captain was so mortified by his error of judgement that he refused to leave the ship or to answer any questions.

Today the remains of the ship still lie on the sands above the high-water mark, and have become something of a tourist attraction.

The first official reference to Noordhoek was in 1743, as part of a farm known as Slangkop ('Snake Head'), occupied by Christina Diemer, the widow of Frederick Rossouw. In 1873 the area was divided into six lots, and the farmers concentrated mainly on growing vegetables to supply ships calling at Simon's Town.

Initially, the name of the area was possibly Noorhoek ('Norwegian Corner'), since the mountains of the southern Peninsula were known as the 'Mountains of Norway'.

In 1902, an article in the *Wynberg Times* described the village and its surroundings. The writer mentions 'nice farm-houses scattered all over, surrounded by cultivated gardens growing nearly every kind of vegetable'. He saw the wreck of the steamship *Kakapo*, and was impressed by the long, white beach. He concluded that Noordhoek was one of the most attractive places he had ever seen.

Kommetjie ('small basin' in Afrikaans) is a village clustered around a small, basin-like inlet on the Atlantic coast. There is evidence that it was used by prehistoric peoples as a natural fish trap. Some of the Khoisan people lived on Slangkop, the mountain that overlooks Kommetjie. The village itself, like Noordhoek, has its origins in a grant of land made in the middle of the eighteenth century to Christina Diemer.

Lord Charles Somerset, Governor of the Cape from 1814 to 1826, had a hunting lodge here. This building is now known as Honeysuckle Cottage.

The village is close to the Slangkop lighthouse. which was built in an attempt to reduce the number of shipwrecks in the area. Slangkop was commissioned in 1914, but not completed until 1919, and is the tallest cast-iron lighthouse on the South African coast. Today, Kommetjie is best known for its excellent surfing.

Kommetjie was relatively isolated until the early years of the twentieth centry, when a road was built around Slangkop. The image below shows the road under construction. Until that time, the only access to Kommetjie (and to the rest of the Noordhoek valley) was via a track over the Steenberg, along which the road now known as Ou Kaapse Weg ('Old Cape Road') was later constructed.

The Slangkop road provides a delightful view of the village, and across Chapman's Bay to Hout Bay and the back of Table Mountain.

Cape Point, a nature reserve covering almost 8 000 hectares, is home to a rich diversity of fauna and flora, including many fynbos species of the Cape Floral Kingdom. Cape Point is part of the Table Mountain National Park, which has been declared a UNESCO World Heritage Site. Both the old and the new lighthouses can be seen in this photograph: the 1860 lighthouse stands poised on Vasco da Gama Peak, and the 1919 lighthouse, much lower down, on Dias Point.

The 'new' lighthouse at Cape Point is a reminder that the rocky headland is renowned for more than its scenic beauty. From the 1400s, when Bartolomeu Dias named it the 'Cape of Storms', Cape Point has been a landmark for seafarers. Many ships have been wrecked on the rocky coastline over the centuries, and the remains of some of these wrecks can still be seen.

The original lighthouse at Cape Point was completed in 1860 and stood on the highest point of Vasco da Gama Peak (opposite page, left and right). However, its height above sea level meant that the light was often obscured by mist or fog. When, on 18 April 1911, the Portuguese liner *Lusitania* ran aground on Bellows Rock, with the loss of eight lives, it was decided to build a new lighthouse on Dias Point, only some 80 metres above sea level (above and opposite page, below).

The foundation stone of the new lighthouse was laid on 25 April 1914, and the lamp was first lit at sunset on 11 March 1919. This is the most powerful light on the South African coast and is visible from a distance of 34 nautical miles.

Cape Point, seen from the sea on a calm day. The Point was treated with great respect by mariners, who knew how dangerous it was, especially in foggy or stormy weather conditions. Contrary to what many people believe, this is not the meeting point of the Atlantic and Indian oceans. The cold Benguela current meets the warm Agulhas current at a point which fluctuates between Cape Point and Cape Agulhas.

The development of Simon's Town (sometimes referred to as Simonstown) owes much to the fact that it is a safe natural harbour. In 1671, a Dutch ship, the *Ysselsteijn*, sheltered here from strong winds, and the captain reported the fact to the Dutch authorities in Batavia (Java). The bay, initially known as Ysselsteijn's Bay, was surveyed by Simon van der Stel, the Governor of the Cape, in 1682, and renamed Simon's Bay.

When the British took over the Cape for the second time, in 1805, their naval establishment was first based in Table Bay, but because Simon's Bay offered a safe anchorage all year round the fleet was transferred to Simon's Town in 1813.

Skilled Malay artisans came to work in Simon's Town, and this was the beginning of the community which became known as Blacktown. In 1904 black workers were employed to build the East Dockyard and the Selborne Dry Docks, and were housed in Luyola ('place of beauty' in Xhosa) on the slopes of Red Hill. In the late 1960s, apartheid regulations led to the forced removal of 'non-white' residents to Ocean View, on the western side of the Peninsula.

Simon's Town was the strategic base for the Royal Navy's South Atlantic Station through both world wars. The base remained under British control until it was handed over to the South African Navy in 1957.

View across Simon's Bay, circa 1910, probably taken from Blacktown, showing ships of the Royal Navy and smaller craft at anchor.

An aerial ropeway once ran between the Simon's Town naval dockyard and the heights above the town. Work began on the ropeway in 1903. It was intended to transport patients, other passengers and stores from the West Dockyard to the naval hospital and sanatorium on Red Hill. The lower station was in the West Dockyard, the intermediate stop was at the Naval Hospital, and the terminus was the summit of Red Hill.

Initially the ropeway ran on wooden pylons, but these were replaced with steel in 1913. The engine house stood next to the Naval Hospital. The ropeway was first powered by a diesel motor and later by electricity.

The journey took 15 minutes, passing over St George's Street on the way to the top station, and the passenger car could carry up to six passengers and an attendant. A goods car was used when stores were transported.

Mr Tom Downie was in charge of the ropeway from 1904, when it began operating, until 1927, when it stopped running. The ropeway was demolished in 1934, and only the small waiting room at the dockyard has been preserved.

Although over a hundred years separate these two photographs, the view is still substantially the same, even to the dormer windows and chimney pots of the former Dockyard Police building.

BRITISH
HOTEL
fresco

The British Hotel, opposite the main entrance to the Simon's Town naval dockyard, is a reminder of Victorian days. This is the second hotel to be built on the site, and dates from 1898. After years of deterioration, a major fire and vandalism, the building was restored in 1991 to its former splendour.

ST GEORGE'S
SALOON BAR UPSTAIRS

The main road through Simon's Town changes its name several times. On entering the town it is called Station Road, thereafter becoming St George Street, and then finally Queen Street. A statue of the famous dog Just Nuisance stands in Jubilee Square, previously Market Square, which is to the right of these photographs. The trees in St George Street had been replaced with palm trees by the 1950s.

JUST NUISANCE

THE STORY OF JUST NUISANCE, the Great Dane who enlisted in the Royal Navy, is well known. His papers show that he 'volunteered' on 6 June 1939 for 'the period of the present emergency' (the Second World War). His trade was given as 'bonecrusher' and his religion as 'scavenger'.

He accompanied sailors who travelled by train from Simon's Town to Cape Town for a night out, and escorted them back when the pubs closed. On one occasion he saved the life of a sailor who had been attacked, barking at a taxi driver until the man realised that Nuisance wanted him to follow. Seeing the sailor lying unconscious, the taxi driver called an ambulance, and the sailor was taken to hospital, with Nuisance in attendance.

Nuisance was discharged from the service on 1 January 1944. He was gradually becoming paralysed as a result of a thrombosis. His condition continued to worsen until a veterinary surgeon advised that he be euthanised. He was buried at Klaver Camp, on nearby Red Hill, with full naval honours.

The bronze statue of Just Nuisance, weighing 75 kilograms, was commissioned by the Simon's Town municipality. The work of local sculptor Jean Doyle, the statue on Jubilee Square was unveiled on 12 July 1985. The square was named in 1935 in honour of King George V's Silver Jubilee.

This view of Main Road, Kalk Bay, shows the Dutch Reformed church on the right. Kalk Bay, a natural harbour noted by Simon van der Stel in the 1680s, took its name from the many lime kilns established in the area (*kalk* is the Dutch word for lime). Lime burning began here in the 1670s, using the mussel shells and other seashells which lay on the beach. The free burghers who ran this enterprise sold the lime to the Dutch East India Company for use in construction work, charging three guilders a ton.

Kalk Bay also became a major fishing centre. Fish was caught and transported to Cape Town, where it formed the staple diet of the slaves. From about 1740, marine stores were transported from Cape Town to Kalk Bay by ox-wagon. From Kalk Bay these stores were conveyed by coaster to Simon's Bay, which had become the winter anchorage for Company ships. In the early 1800s, a whaling station was established here.

Initially, in the 1840s, Dutch Reformed services were held in a private home and led by ministers from Wynberg. Kalk Bay was later incorporated into the Simon's Town congregation, services being held in the hall of the Anglican Church. In 1875 the Dutch Reformed Church bought three lots of ground in Kalk Bay and on 26 April 1876 the small Dutch Reformed church was consecrated. Morning service was conducted by Dr EP Faure in Dutch, and the afternoon service by Dr Robertson in English.

The final service was held on 7 January 1950. The church building was sold and rezoned for business. Subsequently it housed various commercial enterprises and is now the Kalk Bay Theatre.

The busy scene on the beach at Kalk Bay in the early years of the twentieth century is in strong contrast with its appearance today. The present fishing harbour, with its breakwater and lighthouse, is a popular tourist attraction.

Whaling took place at Kalk Bay from the early 1800s. The huge southern right whale yielded, on average, 70 barrels of oil. The vats used to store the whale oil are clearly visible in early photographs. Whale bones were used for furniture and for fencing, and were also exported for use in corsets, shoehorns and umbrellas. In the mid-1820s, about 30 whales were killed and processed each season. (The season ran from August to November each year.)

In the 1840s, the fishing community at Kalk Bay was augmented by groups of emancipated slaves, many of whom had come originally from fishing communities in the East Indies. In the 1870s groups of Filipino sailors who had deserted from American ships also made this their home. The small bay became the centre of a fishing industry, the remnants of which still survive.

In the mid-1800s Kalk Bay became a fashionable resort, and in April 1851 was described in *The Cape Monitor* as a 'salubrious and fashionable watering-place – the Brighton of the Cape'. The railway arrived on 5 May 1883, and this brought even more holidaymakers. In 1889 work began on the extension of the line to Clovelly. A stone viaduct was constructed, effectively cutting Fishery Beach in half and preventing fishermen from pulling their boats onto the shore.

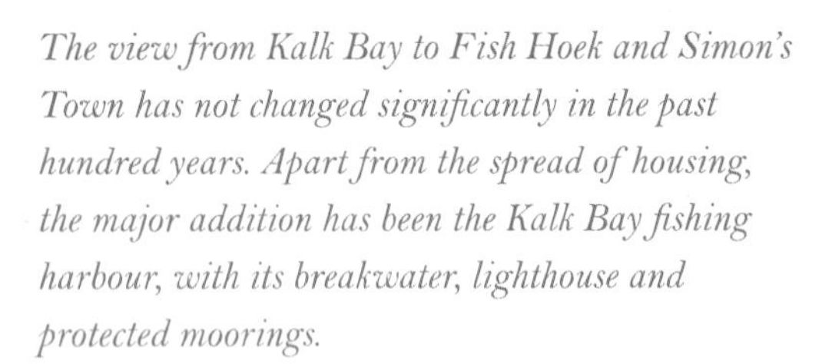

The view from Kalk Bay to Fish Hoek and Simon's Town has not changed significantly in the past hundred years. Apart from the spread of housing, the major addition has been the Kalk Bay fishing harbour, with its breakwater, lighthouse and protected moorings.

ST. JAMES HOTEL
REFRESHMENTS

ST JAMES HOTEL

THE COASTAL VILLAGE OF ST JAMES became a popular holiday resort for Cape Town's elite in the early twentieth century. The St James Hotel, shown here circa 1910, was originally a large private residence named Le Rivage. A number of great cedar trees shaded the front of the house, one of which survived to the 1960s.

Situated right opposite St James station, the hotel was very popular with visitors because it was sheltered from the southeasterly wind.

Shortly after the Second Anglo-Boer War (1899–1902), the owner of the hotel, Captain Gently, began advertising dances 'in the cool sea breezes' with 'first class floor, orchestra, bar and catering arrangements'. A number of guests travelled by train to these events, and Captain Gentry made a habit of serving coffee and biscuits to the stationmaster and the driver of the last train, as he accompanied his guests to the station. Today, the much-enlarged hotel is a retirement home.

Visible at the left of both photographs is St James Roman Catholic church, which was built in the 1880s. The parish of St James was established in 1859, and gave its name to the area.

Muizenberg began as an outpost on the banks of Zandvlei. Het Posthuys ('the posthouse'), a tollhouse established here in 1673 by the Dutch East India Company, is considered one of the oldest buildings in South Africa. In 1743 a military post was established, and Wynand Muys, the sergeant in charge, gave his name to the area. Barracks, stables and a magazine were constructed. These buildings were later used by the British, and the ruins could still be seen in the early years of the twentieth century.

In the days of the Dutch East India Company, Muizenberg was known as a refreshment stop for those travelling from Cape Town to Simon's Town. The Battle of Muizenberg, on 7 April 1795, when the British defeated the Dutch forces, marked the beginning of the first British occupation of the Cape. At this time there were only a handful of farms and a few fishing huts at Muizenberg.

From these small beginnings, Muizenberg developed into a holiday destination and an attractive suburb of Cape Town, which had the distinction of being the first to have a bus service (1902), a permanent cinema (the Electric Theatre, 1902) and airmail delivery of post (1911). In recent years, the face of Muizenberg has changed considerably. However, the sweep of its great beach – 'white as sand of Muizenberg', in the words of poet Rudyard Kipling – remains its greatest asset.

RHODES' COTTAGE

CAPE PREMIER CECIL JOHN RHODES bought this cottage in 1899 to use as a retreat in the hot summer months. Even when it was oppressively hot at his official residence, there were always cool sea breezes at Muizenberg.

Rhodes was ill when he returned (against the advice of his doctors) to the Cape in 1902 after a visit to England, and asked to be moved to his cottage where it would be a little cooler. Unfortunately the weather that year was unusually hot, so he had no relief from the intense heat. He died at his cottage on 26 March 1902.

During Rhodes' ownership, the cottage had a corrugated-iron roof with dormer windows at the front. After his death, the front dormers were removed and the corrugated iron replaced with thatch.

The cottage was unoccupied until 1932, when the Rhodes Trust gave it to the Northern Rhodesian government. Five years later, it was returned to the Cape Town city council as a gift. It was declared a heritage site the following year, and in 1953 was converted into a museum

Muizenberg's fine bathing beach became its greatest attraction in the 1890s, but its days as a seaside resort began in the 1820s, when Farmer Peck's Inn became one of the first seaside hotels in the Cape.

Thousands of people travelled to Muizenberg on public holidays. After the Second Anglo-Boar War (1899–1902), it became such a popular destination that direct trains ran from Johannesburg, via a loop at Salt River, to Muizenberg station. In 1902 the jumble of private bathing huts was removed, and the municipality erected a neat row of bathing boxes. The amenities were completed by the building of a wooden pavilion in 1910.

A guidebook of 1914 describes the resort in glowing terms: 'The sea is the complete renovator. It is the only cure-of-all-aches, there is nothing so tonic as a dip ... and nothing so calculated to revive the sense of well-being than ... to spend lazy hours on the Muizenberg sands.'

A tourist brochure of 1918 extolled the health benefits of surfing: 'It steadies the nerves, exercises the muscles, and makes the enthusiast clear headed and clear eyed.' Surfing is still a popular sport at Muizenberg today, particularly at Surfer's Corner (shown above), where the slow, gentle waves are ideal for novices.

KIRSTENBOSCH

KIRSTENBOSCH NATIONAL BOTANICAL GARDEN, arguably the most beautiful botanical garden in the world, occupies land that was once the property of the Dutch East India Company, which used it mainly as a source of timber. In 1660, Jan van Riebeeck planted a hedge of indigenous wild almonds to mark the boundary of the colony. Parts of this hedge still exist today. The land was acquired by Cecil John Rhodes in the 1890s and bequeathed to the nation.

The garden was established through the efforts of botanist Henry Harold Welch Pearson. Born in England in 1870, Pearson came to the Cape in 1903 as the first Professor of Botany at the South African College (later the University of Cape Town). He decided that the farm Kirstenbosch provided an ideal situation for a botanic garden. In 1913, after years of campaigning and planning, the government finally agreed to this, and voted an annual grant of £1 000. Pearson was appointed the garden's first director.

Kirstenbosch's goal is to preserve South Africa's indigenous flora. One way it does this is by making plants available to the public. The images at left show nursery plants for sale. On the opposite page is shown a labourer's cottage at what is now the entrance to the garden (top), the Director's house (bottom left) and the modern interpretive centre (bottom, right).

KIRSTENBOSCH

When Henry Pearson was appointed director of Kirstenbosch, he began clearing the area with his staff. His position carried no salary, so he was able to work on the garden only on Wednesdays and weekends. For the rest of the week he was fully occupied by his duties as Professor of Botany.

He died of pneumonia in 1916 and was buried at Kirstenbosch. His grave (left and below) is marked by a granite cross with the inscription 'If ye seek his monument, look around'.

Kirstenbosch has grown over the years and the estate now covers over 500 hectares, of which about 40 hectares is cultivated garden, and the remainder natural forest and fynbos.

GROOTE SCHUUR HOSPITAL

GROOTE SCHUUR HOSPITAL is an impressive Cape Town landmark, both geographically and historically. Its origins lie in the first land grants made by the Dutch East India Company to free burghers along the Liesbeeck River. 'De Schuur' (later known as 'de Groote Schuur', meaning 'the large barn') was built in 1657 for the storage of the grain produced by these farmers.

Cecil John Rhodes secured extensive land holdings between Kirstenbosch and Observatory in 1893. He built a large house on the site of the old barn, and left it to the government, to be a home for the country's prime ministers. He bequeathed the remainder of his estate to 'a united South Africa', expressing the wish that some of the land be used for a university.

In 1918, the University of Cape Town was established on one part of the estate, and a special act, passed in 1920, sanctioned the building of a hospital on the northern portion of the site. The University agreed to lease 11 hectares of land, next to the new Medical School, to the Cape Hospital Board for 99 years. This land was intended for a new teaching hospital for the University's Faculty of Medicine. In 1929, it was decided to build a hospital with 850 beds on the site at a cost of £750 000, to be known as Groote Schuur Hospital.

The building was designed by the architect of the Department of Public Works, Mr FD Strong. The foundation stones were laid in 1932, and three years later the Hospital Board appealed to the citizens of Cape Town for funds for equipment. The response was overwhelming, and £75 000 was raised.

On 31 January 1939 the new hospital was officially opened, although there were only enough nursing staff for 450 beds. Only in the 1940s did the hospital begin to function at full capacity.

Well-positioned on the slopes of Devil's Peak, the building was a symphony of cream walls, roofs of red tiles, cupolas and statuary, finished with striking teak shutters (which unfortunately were later removed). The rich decorative detail and superb craftsmanship remind us of a more gracious age.

Groote Schuur Hospital, now greatly enlarged, is perhaps best known as the facility in which the first heart transplant, under the leadership of Dr Christiaan Barnard, took place in 1967.

In 1897, a company named Milnerton Estates Ltd purchased the properties known as Paarden Island and Jan Biesjes Kraal, with the intention of laying out a township to be known as Milnerton, in honour of Lord Milner, the British High Commissioner. A railway line, connecting the new township with Cape Town, was also planned.

It was only in 1903 that the first plots were put up for sale by public auction. On Boxing Day in the same year, the first trains ran from Cape Town station to Milnerton, and in 1904 regular services were introduced. A tea bungalow, concert hall and dancing pavilion were among the attractions offered to visitors. Further plots were auctioned in 1905. A racecourse was the next amenity to be suggested, and the first race took place on 28 May 1908.

The new township was popular, being both close to the city and affordable. From its beginnings as a tranquil residential township, it has grown into a bustling suburb of Cape Town.

The beach at Milnerton is popular with walkers and surfers, and offers a panoramic view across the bay to Table Mountain.

The Diep River flows through the Rietvlei Wetland Reserve to Milnerton Lagoon and the sea. This reserve is one of the most important sites for waterbirds in the region, owing to the wide range of wetland habitats and the proximity of the sea. Stretches of typical Strandveld flora and fauna flourish where alien vegetation has been removed.

The beach at Blouberg affords one of the most famous views of Cape Town and Table Mountain. Many ships have been lost at Blouberg over the years, although few wrecks resulted in any loss of life. The earliest recorded wreck was that of the Sévere, *a French man-of-war transporting soldiers from Mauritius to France, on 27 January 1784. In the 1800s a number of ships were wrecked: the* Cerberus, *on a voyage from Ceylon to London, was lost on 10 March 1821, and the* John *was lost on 4 December that year, although her cargo of spices and coffee was saved. The* Sappho, *on a voyage from Shanghai to London with a cargo of 600 tons of tea, was lost during a gale on 15 March 1864. A Russian ship,* Onni, *was wrecked on 7 February 1890. She was carrying a cargo of coal for the Gas Light Company.*

On 9 October 1896, the Norwegian ship Atlas, *a wooden ship of 1 296 tons under the command of Captain JL Marchussen, was wrecked on Blouberg Beach. She was carrying a cargo of teak from Asia. The* Armenia, *an Italian barque under the command of Captain Schaffina, collided with another vessel at the start of her voyage from Cape Town. The ship anchored off Blouberg, but then ran ashore on 9 June 1902 during a storm.*

The most recent wreck at Blouberg was that of the Seli 1, *a Turkish bulk carrier, which ran aground on 8 September 2009. The unsightly wreck lay just offshore for four years before explosives were used to collapse it onto the sea bed.*

The first documented mention of Robben Island was by the Portuguese explorer Vasco da Gama, who landed on the island in 1496 to slaughter seals for their meat and oil. From the 1500s the island was a regular port of call for seafarers who needed to replenish their stores.

By 1654 there was a small community on the island. Shepherds cared for small flocks of sheep and goats, shelters were built, and a vegetable garden started. The first group of prisoners (slaves and exiles) were sent to the island in 1657 and worked at quarrying limestone and slate. In the eighteenth century the prison population consisted of political prisoners banished from their native countries in the East Indies for resisting Dutch rule, as well as pirates and bandits.

In the 1800s, under British rule, the island was not only used as a prison. It was the site of a whaling station and a stone quarry, and persons with infectious diseases were quarantined there.

In the 1840s many of the criminal prisoners were returned to the mainland, where they were put to work as labourers, constructing roads, and maintaining passes and bridges in the Cape Colony.

The lighthouse on the island, designed by the Colonial Engineer John Scott Tucker and built in 1865, was constructed from locally quarried stone. In the second half of the nineteenth century a hospital, known as the General Infirmary, was built on the island to house lepers, lunatics and paupers.

In 1875 the island had a population of 552, according to the census returns. By 1891 this figure had risen to 702, and by 1904 the population was 1 460.

In the early twentieth century the chronic sick were gradually removed to the mainland, and in the 1920s the mental patients were transferred to Valkenberg Asylum. The leper hospital was closed in 1931.

For some years after this, Robben Island was largely abandoned. When the Second World War broke out, it was decided to fortify the island against possible attack and two gun batteries were constructed. Thousands of troops, including women of the Women's Auxiliary Army Corps and the South African Women's Auxiliary Naval Service, were stationed on the island throughout the war. Subsequently, from 1946, a Permanent Force unit, the Coastal Artillery School, was established on the island and army gunners and their families settled there. When the School became a branch of the navy in the 1950s, the island became a navy training base known as SAS *Robbeneiland.*

In the 1960s the island once again became a prison. Following the Rivonia Trial, the senior leadership of the banned African National Congress (ANC), including Nelson Mandela, Walter Sisulu, Govan Mbeki and Ahmed Kathrada, were sent here. Also imprisoned was Robert Sobukwe, the leader of the banned Pan Africanist Congress (PAC), who was kept in a small cottage isolated from contact with other prisoners. Conditions on the island were harsh and unrelenting, with the political prisoners compelled to labour in the island's limestone quarry. Convicted criminals were housed in a separate facility.

Change was a long time in coming, and it was only in the 1980s that Mandela and other high-profile prisoners were transferred to facilities on the mainland. Mandela walked out from Victor Verster prison, outside Paarl, a free man again, in February 1990, and by the end of 1991 the remaining political prisoners on Robben Island had been released. The island continued to house convicted criminals until 1996.

Today Robben Island is a museum commemorating the injustices of the past and is visited by tens of thousands of people each year. In 1999 it was declared a UNESCO World Heritage Site.

p 1: Kalk Bay beach, c. 1882 **M672**

pp 2–3: View of Devil's Peak, Table Mountain and Signal Hill, undated **J5054**

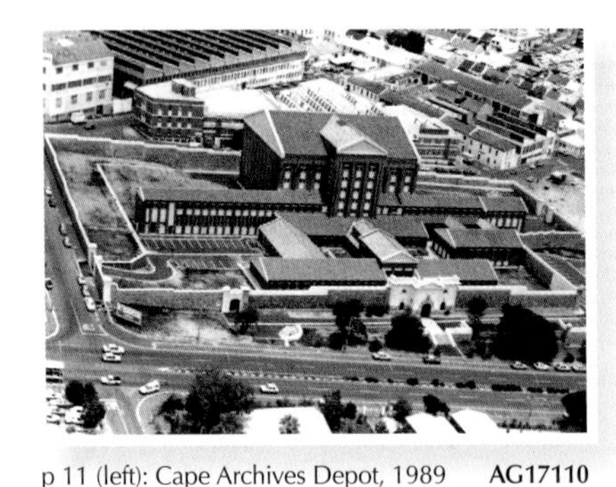

p 11 (left): Cape Archives Depot, 1989 **AG17110**

p 11 (right): Roeland Street Prison, 1977 **AG17501**

p 14 (top): Roggebaai, undated **S80**

p 14 (bottom): Roggebaai, undated **R1570**

p 16: Table Mountain, undated **R1578**

p 18 (top): Table Bay, undated **R1575**

p 18 (bottom): Table Bay, undated **S78**

p 20: The Castle of Good Hope, undated **E8134**

p 22: The Grand Parade and City Hall, undated **AG985**

pp 24–25: Adderley Street, undated **R1089**

p 26: Standard Bank Building, undated **AG12977**

pp 28–29: Adderley Street, 1905 **E7863**

p 30 (top): The Pier, c. 1920 **R1642**

p 30 (bottom): The Pier, c. 1920 **R1645**

p 31: The Pier, undated **AG4647**

p 32: The Pier and Jan van Riebeeck statue, c. 1920 **R1009**

pp 32–33: Jan van Riebeeck statue, undated **E9339**

p 34: Table Bay docks, c.1900 **S82**

pp 36–37: Horse-drawn drays in Table Bay harbour, c.1896 **J8135**

p 38: Argentine Training Ship, undated **E8070**

p 40: The Clock Tower, undated **S81**

pp 42–43: Central Cape Town, 1890 **H57**

pp 44–45: Greenmarket Square, undated **AG979**

pp 46–47: Greenmarket Square, c.1881 **E2072**

pp 48–49: Strand Street, 1900 **M674**

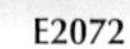

pp 54–55: Lion's Head and Signal Hill, c.1890 **H51**

p 56: Military Camp, Green Point, c.1900 **R1443**

p 50: Bo-Kaap, undated **E2030**

pp 58–59: British camp on Green Point Common, c.1900 **E7826**

p 62: Beach Road, Mouille Point, undated **AG3473**

p 64: Wreck of the *Thermopylae*, 1899 **DrJ73**

p 66: Three Anchor Bay, undated **E2132**

pp 68–69: Steam train at Sea Point, undated **R1145**

p 70: Queen's Hotel, Sea Point, c. 1910 **AG3467**

pp 72–73: Bantry Bay, undated **S125**

p 74: Clifton, c. 1902 **S90**

pp 76–77: Clifton, undated **E2954**

p 78: Clifton Hotel, c. 1902 **R1053**

p 80: Tram in Camps Bay, undated **J10295**

pp 82–83: Tram route from Kloof Nek to Camps Bay, undated **R1452**

pp 84–85: Victoria Road, Camps Bay, c.1880 **AG14956**

p 88: Llandudno from Victoria Road, 1893 **DrJ179**

p 90: Hout Bay, c.1900 **S98**

pp 92–93: Hout Bay at the turn of the century, undated **AG996**

p 94: East Fort, Hout Bay, undated **AG14964**

p 96: Wreck of the *Kakapo*, 1903 **AG6571**

p 98: Noordhoek, undated **CA1652**

p 100: Kommetjie, undated **G246**

p 102: New road to Kommetjie, undated **G248**

p 106: Cape Point lighthouse, c. 1920 **E8667**

p 110: Simon's Town, c. 1900 **R1491**

p 120: Just Nuisance, c. 1940 **G295**

pp 112–113: Simon's Bay, undated **E8086**

p 114: Aerial ropeway, Simon's Town, c. 1915 **G582**

pp 118–119: St George Street, Simon's Town, undated **R1135**

p 122: Main Road, Kalk Bay, undated **R1017**

pp 124–125: Kalk Bay, c.1900 **E9337**

p 126: Kalk Bay beach, undated **R1019**

p 128: Kalk Bay and Simon's Town, undated **R1018**

p 130: St James Hotel, c. 1910 **R1116**

p 132: Muizenberg, c. 1900 **R1136**

p 134: Rhodes' cottage, c.1900 **J9573**

p 136: Muizenberg beach, c. 1912 **E7565**

p 138: Nursery, undated **E5879**

p 139 (top): Labourer's cottage, undated **S69**

p 139 (bottom left): Director's house, undated **E5897**

p 140: Grave of Henry Pearson, undated **E5879**

p 142: Groote Schuur Hospital, undated **E1334**

p 144: Table Mountain from Milnerton, undated **E5758**

pp 146–147: Shipwreck at Blouberg beach, undated **E7948**

p 148 (top left): Robben Island lighthouse, 1899 **DrJ764**

p 148 (top right): Table Mountain from Robben Island, undated **E8147**

p 148 (bottom): The wharf at Robben Island, 1898 **DrJ1022**

BOOKS and JOURNALS

—, 1825. *The African Court Calendar and Directory.* Cape Town: Colonial Printing Office.

—, 1881. *The Cape of Good Hope Almanac.* Cape Town: Government Printer.

—, 1968. In Memoriam – Miss M K Jeffreys. *Archives News,* Vol 9, No 2, pp 41–44.

Athiros, G and Athiros, L [eds], 2007. *Woodstock – a selection of articles from the Woodstock Whisperer.* Cape Town: Historical Media cc.

Bickford-Smith, V, van Heyningen, E and Worden, N, 1999. *Cape Town in the twentieth century.* Claremont: David Philip.

Burman, J, 1977. *The False Bay story.* Cape Town: Human & Rousseau.

City of Cape Town, 2009. *Beaches – a diversity of coastal treasures.* Cape Town: City of Cape Town.

Davids, A, 1980. *The mosques of Bo-Kaap.* Claremont: Institute of Arabic and Islamic Research.

De Beer, M, 1987. *The Lion Mountain.* Cape Town: AA Balkema.

De Beer, M, 1992. *A vision of the past – South Africa in photographs 1843–1910.* Cape Town: Struik.

Dommisse, B and Westby-Nunn, A, 2002. *Simonstown – an illustrated historical perspective.* Cape Town: Westby-Nunn Publishers cc.

eGGSA, 2004. Charles Hopkins. *Genesis.* 40th anniversary special edition. Available at <http://www.eggsa.org/genesis_40_download_e.htm> [Accessed 10 January 2012]

Fransen, H, 1969. *The architectural beauty of the old Cape as seen by Arthur Elliott.* Cape Town: AA Balkema.

Green, L, 1951. *Growing lovely, growing old. Cape Town:* Howard Timmins.

Krumm, HE [ed], 1944. *Monthly notes of the Astronomical Society of South Africa,* Vol 3, No 7, p 1.

Krynauw, DW and Möller, GSJ, 1994. *Blouberg – ons beroemdste strand.* Cape Town: Human & Rousseau.

Leverton, BJ, 1972. A Ravenscroft Vignette. *Archives News,* Vol 24, No 7, pp 23–24.

Midgley, JF, 1975. *Kommetjie, C.P. – its story.* Privately printed.

Mienie, JH, 1984. Argivaris van Kaapse Ned. Geref. Kerk tree af. *Archives News,* Vol 24, No 2, pp 15–16.

Muir, J, 1975. *Know your Cape.* Cape Town: Howard Timmins.

Murray, M, 1964. *Under Lion's Head.* Cape Town: AA Balkema.

Newall, P, 1993. *Cape Town harbour 1652 to the present.* Portnet.

Pakenham, T, 1979. *The Boer War.* Johannesburg: Jonathan Ball.

Potgieter, DJ [ed], 1972. *Standard Encyclopaedia of Southern Africa.* Cape Town: Nasou Ltd.

Rosenthal, E, 1977. *Fish horns and hansom cabs.* Johannesburg: AD Donker Pty Ltd.

Rosenthal, E, 1980. *History of Milnerton.* Cape Town: Milnerton Municipality.

Standard Bank, 2009. *Historical overview.* Available at <http://www.standardbank.com/history.aspx> [Accessed 9 March 2013]

Steyn, LM, 1968. *Just Nuisance.* Spectrum Publishing Company.

Turner, M, 1988. *Shipwreck and salvage in South Africa.* Cape Town: Struik.

Van der Merwe, J, 1985. The Elliot Photograph collection. *Archives News,* Vol 27, No 27, pp 28–30.

Van Rensburg, R, 1980–1. Miss M K Jeffreys. *Archives News,* Vol 24, No 1, pp 11–13.

Walker, M, 1997. *The golden years.* Privately printed.

Walker, M, 2002. *Kalk Bay – a place of character.* Cape Town: City Graphics.

Walker, M, 2009. *Muizenberg – a forgotten story.* Cape Town: Michael Walker.

Westby-Nunn, T, 2005. *Hout Bay – an illustrated historical profile.* Cape Town: Westby-Nunn Publishers cc.

Wexham, B, undated. S*hipwrecks of the Western Cape.* Cape Town: Howard Timmins.

Wolfaardt, A, 1961. Die Ravenscroft-versameling van negatiewe. *Archives News,* Vol 5, No 6, pp 16–19.

Worden, N, van Heyningen, E and Bickford-Smith, V, 1998. *Cape Town – the making of a city.* Claremont: David Philip.

ARCHIVAL DOCUMENTS

Chief, Cape Archives Depot: C3/15/29, C3/15/31, C3/15/163

Colonial Office: CO 4237:S63, CO 4273:S35

Master of the Orphan Chamber: 6/9/5190:61950, 6/9/10946:92424, 6/9/14878:1624

Master of the Supreme Court: 3893/68, 1237/93

WEBSITES

Baillie-Cooper, S, 2004. *Lighthouses of South Africa.* Available at <http://www.lighthouses.co.za> [Accessed 22 March 2013]

Camps Bay Community, 2001. *Camps Bay tramways.* Available at <http://www.campsbaycommunity.com/heritage-cameos/camps-bay-tramways/> [Accessed 23 February 2013]

Camps Bay Community, 2001. *The Rotunda.* Available at <http://www.campsbaycommunity.com/heritage-cameos/the-rotunda/> [Accessed 23 February 2013]

Kane-Berman, J, undated. *Groote Schuur Hospital: historical perspective.* Available at <https://www.gshfb.co.za/index.php.about-the-board> [Accessed 22 March 2013]

Kommetjie Online, 2013. *History of Kommetjie.* Available at <http://kommetjie-online.co.za/history.html> [Accessed 28 March 2013]

Maude, S, 2003. *Llandudno – early history.* Available at <http://www.llandudno.co.za/area-guide/llandudno-history/early-history.html> [Accessed 1 April 2013]

South African History Online, undated. *Cape Town.* Available at <http://www.sahistory.org.za/places/cape-town> [Accessed February and March 2013]

Cape Town history – a tourist guide. Available at <http://capetownhistory.co.za> [Accessed February and March 2013]

First published in 2013 by Struik Travel & Heritage
(an imprint of Random House Struik (Pty) Ltd)
Company Reg. No. 1966/003153/07
Wembley Square, First Floor, Solan Road, Gardens, Cape Town 8001
PO Box 1144, Cape Town 8000, South Africa

www.randomstruik.co.za

Publisher: Pippa Parker
Managing editor: Roelien Theron
Editor: Alfred LeMaitre
Designer: Janice Evans
Project coordinator: Alana Bolligelo
Proofreader: Trish Myers Smith

Reproduction by Hirt & Carter Cape (Pty) Ltd
Printing and binding: Toppan Leefung Packaging and Printing (Dongguan) Co., Ltd, China

ISBN 978 1 92054 591 8 (Print)
ISBN 978 1 92054 592 5 (ePub)
ISBN 978 1 92054 593 2 (PDF)

10 9 8 7 6 5 4 3 2 1

Please email any comments to:
ct_thenandnow@randomstruik.co.za

Get monthly updates and news by subscribing to our newsletter at **www.randomstruik.co.za**